THE JESUS WAY

The Jesus Way

A CONVERSATION ON THE WAYS
THAT JESUS IS THE WAY

Eugene H. Peterson

WILLIAM B. EERDMANS PUBLISHING COMPANY
GRAND RAPIDS, MICHIGAN / CAMBRIDGE, U.K.

Published 2007 by
Wm. B. Eerdmans Publishing Co.
2140 Oak Industrial Drive N.E., Grand Rapids, Michigan 49505 /
P.O. Box 163, Cambridge CB3 9PU U.K.
www.eerdmans.com

Published in association with the literary agency of
Alive Communications, Inc.,
7680 Goddard Street #200, Colorado Springs, CO 80290

Printed in the United States of America

12 11 10 09 08 07   7 6 5 4 3 2 1

Library of Congress Cataloging-in-Publication Data

Peterson, Eugene H., 1932-
The Jesus way: a conversation on the ways that Jesus is the way /
Eugene H. Peterson.
p.   cm.
ISBN 978-0-8028-2949-8 (cloth : alk. paper)
1. Jesus Christ — Example.   2. Christian life.   3. Christianity and culture.
4. Apologetics.   5. Bible — Criticism, interpretation, etc.   I. Title.

BT304.2.P48   2007
232 — dc22

2006036408

"On Writing Poetry" by John Leax. Copyright © 2004 by John Leax. Originally published in
Grace Is Where I Live by John Leax (La Porte, Ind.: WordFarm, 2004). Used with permission
from WordFarm, www.wordfarm.net.

Unless otherwise noted, Bible quotations in this publication are taken from the New
Revised Standard Version Bible, copyright © 1989, by the Division of Christian Education of
the National Council of the Churches of Christ in the United States of America.

For Michael and Nancy Crowe
Wise companions in the company of men and women
who follow in the way of Jesus